Reading the Wood

May 96

To start you off on the road of creativity and fulfilling days.
With love,
Me.

Michael Elkan

At our home
studio near Silver
Creek Falls in the
foothills of the Oregon
Cascades, we work surrounded
by the trees from which we get
our inspiration — like the creek,
energy flows naturally, is absorbed,
and our work is a reflection of the process.

Reading the Wood

Techniques & Projects from a Master Woodworker

Michael Elkan

Sterling Publishing Co., Inc. New York
A Sterling/Chapelle Book

FOR CHAPELLE:
  Owner: Jo Packham
  Editor: Cathy Sexton
  Staff: Malissa Boatwright, Rebecca Christensen, Kellie Cracas, Holly Hollingsworth, Susan Jorgensen, Susan Laws, Amanda McPeck, Barbara Milburn, Leslie Ridenour, Cindy Rooks, Cindy Stoeckl, and Nancy Whitley
  Photography: Ryne Hazen and Kevin Dilley for Hazen Photography
                    Eric Griswold
  Technical Drawings: Tonner Hays

Photo from page 1:   The title of this sculpture is "The Path Home" — a collaboration with Helen Issifu
Photo from page 3:   The title of this sculpture is "Philadelphia, 1950"
Photo from page 11:   The title of this sculpture is "Castle Number One"
Photo from page 31:   The title of this sculpture is "The Bridge"
Photo from page 49:   The title of this sculpture is "Underwater Life" — collection of Lewis Judy and Toni Gilbert
Photo from page 107:   The title of this sculpture is "Casa de Iguana"

If you have any questions or comments or would like information on specialty products featured in this book, please contact: Chapelle, Ltd., Inc., P.O. Box 9252, Ogden, UT 84409 • (801) 621-2777 • (801) 621-2788 Fax

Library of Congress Cataloging-in-Publication Data
Elkan, Michael, 1942-
        Reading the wood : techniques & projects from a master woodworker / Michael Elkan.
              p.   cm.
        "A Sterling / Chapelle book."
        Includes index.
        ISBN 0-8069-4274-6
        1. Woodwork. 2. Wood—Figure. 3. Elkan, Michael, 1942—
        -Knowledge—Woodwork. I. Title.
        TT200.E43   1996
        730'.028—dc20   95-44149
                                                                             CIP

10 9 8 7 6 5 4 3 2 1

Published by Sterling Publishing Company, Inc.
387 Park Avenue South, New York, NY 10016
© 1996 by Chapelle Ltd.
Distributed in Canada by Sterling Publishing
c/o Canadian Manda Group, One Atlantic Avenue, Suite 105
Toronto, Ontario, Canada M6K 3E7
Distributed in Great Britain and Europe by Cassell PLC
Wellington House, 125 Strand, London WC2R 0BB, England
Distributed in Australia by Capricorn Link (Australia) Pty Ltd.
P.O. Box 6651, Baulkham Hills, Business Centre, NSW 2153, Australia
Printed and Bound in Hong Kong
All Rights Reserved

Sterling ISBN-0-8069-4274-6

FOREWORD

Some people spend their whole lives in search of beauty. Others have the gift to see beauty constantly in their everyday surroundings. Michael Elkan is both of these people. He is a seeker who is never content with his past accomplishments, always looking for growth and change. But he also has the gift of finding beauty everywhere. From every person he meets and every place he visits, Michael absorbs energy that he later translates into a sculpture or a piece of furniture.

Michael finds inspiration in every piece of wood he uses. With a great deal of respect for the natural beauty of each piece, he sets out to enhance and share what nature has created. The result is a dining room set with the table and all the chairs created from a single tree, a book-matched coffee table with a gnawed beaver stick incorporated in it, or a sculpture box with each piece placed right where it originally grew. Michael often works with burls and growths that other woodworkers consider undesirable due to their irregular nature. Michael turns that irregularity into a work of art.

Michael came to the craft world in 1979 after leaving behind a successful, but frantic career in the clothing and fabric design industry. He was looking for a different life-style and found it as a self-employed artist living in the scenic, peaceful Oregon country-side. Unlike many artists, Michael had a strong foundation in marketing and business skills on which to build a company. He took the old European approach to craft, where he was the de-signer, but used the skills of a studio of workers to complete the product. He also diversified, creating smaller, less expensive boxes and desk accessories and also wonderful one-of-a-kind pieces of furniture. This understanding of retail has kept Michael's studio on a strong economic growth pattern.

Michael's work has always been a pleasure for us to show and sell. In twenty-five years of retailing American craft, we have had the opportunity to work with thousands of artists, many of whom we consider friends. Michael and Sharon Elkan are on the top of that list. We have shared many great times together. In today's crazy world, it is important that we share not only what we can do, but also who we are. The Elkans have done that. Our relationship with Sharon and Michael has definitely enhanced our business and our lives. Their art is a special gift to all who receive it.

Judy and Stan Gillis
Real Mother Goose Gallery
Portland, Oregon

It is spring in Oregon. The people from Chapelle are here to do the photography for this book. In a way it is the perfect Oregon. The mist is so fine you have to look twice to see it and you don't even feel it. Except, you get awfully wet walking through the forest — all the plants are looking up drinking the mist, like manna from Heaven. You can see the bright spot in the sky where the sun just glistens a bit through the solid grey cloud cover. And the green — it's difficult to describe — infinite different shades. This little cleared spot in the mountain's forest, it feels as if the trees and plants want to grow so fast they will cover us up — fold us into an almost warm, moist, womb.

What I'd like to portray in the writing of this book is that there was no master plan and no formula — just a path that was allowed to happen.

The pieces I make are not necessarily planned, they have evolved — and are like discoveries along the path. The story I'd like to tell, is like walking in the creek — it turns, it has tributaries, and it has new discoveries around each bend.

First and foremost, to my beautiful wife, Sharon — my companion on the path.

ACKNOWLEDGMENTS

To Jules and Frances Elkan, who said if we're to be friends it will be because we love each other, not because we're your parents. They would have loved to see this book.

To Aaron Frank and Harold Oppenhiem, my mentors, who gave me my first opportunity to design.

To Pat and Sally Paszkiewicz, who taught us how to live in the woods and so much more.

To Russell Swider, who saw some potential in me and made me buy my first bandsaw. He then continued to encourage me to show my work for the first time.

To Ken Altman, the consummate craftsman.

To Norman Flakser, who made the voyage to Oregon with us, and whose humor, insight, and way with words attributed much to the writing of this book.

To Jo Packham and Cathy Sexton, true professionals in the art of producing a book.

To those who came before and created the spirit for this book — George Nakashima and Wharton Esherick.

Our studio is unique. We work together with no set hours or time clocks, and no one in the studio was trained as a woodworker, but all are gems in their own right and make this endeavor possible. Each person offers his own feelings, expertise, and integrity engraved in every piece.

I couldn't even think about writing this book without acknowledging the wonderful people who have worked with me through the years:

Ken and Ann Altman
Neil Austin
David Bosshardt
Beth Chase
Chuck and Mona Elkan
Norman Friedman
Richard Greenman
Howard Griffiths
Helen Issifu
Sue Marcoe
Harry Pendergrass
Lorenzo Rodriguez
Theresa Sharrar
Estebon Soto
Dennis Swanson
Philip Virga

We recycle all glass, plastic, metal, paper, cardboard, sawdust, magazines, and wood scraps and use on-demand solar water heating, wood heat, and energy-efficient lighting.

CONTENTS

Reading the Wood is the goal, to both discover and create. To realize that which is within.

A fisherman may read the water, a pilot might read the sky, a woodworker must read the wood.

PART ONE

The
Path Begins

My father was known as Jules, or Reds — for his flaming, wavy red hair. He left home at about 12 years old and had many jobs during his lifetime.

My mother, Frances, a warm and wonderful person encouraged my limited artistic ability.

FOLLOWING THE PATH

On August 16, 1942, I was the first of three children born to Julius and Frances Elkan. It seems that so much of who I am is derived from my north Philadelphia roots.

One day while driving his cab, my father spotted a store for rent at Front and Allegheny Streets. I was 10 years old when he opened a children's clothing store with $100 and a little credit. We sold seconds, thirds, and fourths of children's socks and underwear. Of course, there is nothing quite like that today. I remember fishing through huge cartons to try and match the socks in size and color. I worked most of my free time — after school and Saturdays. Sundays my father would take me down to 3rd and Market Streets, a stop at Horn and Hardarts Cafeteria, where we would stand and eat breakfast. They used to have those little glass covered boxes and you would put in a nickel or dime, open the door, and have some rice pudding or other small dish. Then, we would make our rounds to the jobbers. With the cash he had collected during the week, he would buy a few more cartons of merchandise.

The lessons I learned were many. In order to make the store look like we had lots of merchandise, he would stack empty boxes upside down.

When I was 18 years old, he said it was time to leave, explaining to me that by that time in his life he had already had 30 jobs and he didn't want this kind of life for me — or for him, for that matter.

His thinking was, from that time on, we were equals. If we really liked each other, we might be friends. If not, I was on my own and could do as I pleased. Jules and I became great friends.

By this time, the rags were in my blood. I went to work as a salesman of frilly dresses and snowsuits — the first of many jobs.

About this time I fell in love and married Sharon — a partnership that meant everything and still does.

A few years passed when my best friend, Sidney, asked me to join him and work for a sweater manufacturer.

I was given a job in "The Big Apple." Shortly, they moved me to the sales office — the 47th floor of the Empire State Building.

Aaron Frank and Harold Oppenheim were the owners of Forum Sportswear, with a supporting cast of fabulous characters. They treated me like a son and were major influences in my life.

One day while at one of the musty old mills, we were taking inventory of yarns the company owned. Quite naively, I asked the mill owner if we could try something different on the knitting machines. We did just that and the skinny ribs were born — V-neck, super tight, and multicolored.

These designs became immensely popular. What a life! Everybody was writing about and selling my designs. I even drove a Porsche — the kid from north Philadelphia had made it. All of the things I learned from Jules, and all of those miserable days spent working after school, were paying off at last.

Instead of my three-piece suit, I wore jeans. The Empire State Building was shocked — in those days, they thought not wearing a hat was crude.

It didn't take long for the concrete jungle, the commuting to New York, the night life, and the constant pressure to take their toll. Exciting as it was, no sooner had a season's styles, fabrics, and colors been put to bed, than the next began — usually three per year.

Other things were becoming more important, so, at the age of 30, I left. Sharon and I were looking for something different.

After selling our house and all of our belongings in Bucks County, Pennsylvania, we spent a fabulous summer with a caravan of friends tripping from Nova Scotia across Canada to, of all places, Oregon!

We had been to Oregon once before on a vacation and it felt like home. At that time, we drove a Rent-A-Wreck for several days and found ourselves at Silver Falls Park, never suspecting it would become our home. Two years later, here we were — back in Oregon.

Each day we would drive the back roads, searching for our vision of where we wanted to live. Rolling hills, running water, trees, and gardens — of course, we were really describing Pennsylvania.

It seemed we had hit every road in the county, until one day I was driving a new road — one I couldn't believe we had missed. It was a tunnel of trees, pouring rain and sleet, and even I knew my dream of building a house was not going to happen in this weather.

MEASURED MONTHLY RAINFALL FOR THE DECADE YEARS 1975 THRU 1984

Annual Average: 101.61 inches

JAN	FEB	MAR	APR	MAY	JUNE	JULY	AUG	SEPT	OCT	NOV	DEC	TOTAL INCHES OF RAINFALL
15.33	10.54	11.21	8.58	5.49	3.27	0.10	5.10	NONE	8.05	12.38	16.69	96.74 (1975)
15.79	12.01	9.26	6.78	5.69	2.62	1.71	4.59	2.30	4.66	1.66	3.68	70.75 (1976)
2.57	9.46	13.96	3.42	10.88	2.01	1.25	3.90	9.20	6.72	17.94	24.11	105.42 (1977)
12.54	8.98	3.90	12.72	7.78	5.97	2.45	6.44	5.66	1.94	10.81	10.10	89.29 (1978)
4.79	23.22	6.81	9.42	5.32	1.57	0.85	2.21	4.35	12.50	9.46	13.74	94.42 (1979)
20.79	8.39	10.14	8.53	4.13	3.28	0.74	0.53	4.78	2.82	17.50	23.32	104.95 (1980)
4.81	10.68	8.30	8.39	6.24	8.14	0.66	0.31	4.87	8.57	13.39	24.67	99.03 (1981)
19.67	16.76	11.73	10.24	1.92	3.17	1.59	2.05	5.22	9.07	11.58	17.13	110.13 (1982)
19.07	16.20	18.18	5.21	7.81	8.52	6.72	3.22	2.01	4.41	21.57	13.24	126.16 (1983)
8.07	13.24	12.35	10.40	10.52	12.77	0.17	0.37	3.81	12.05	25.54	9.94	119.23 (1984)

I stopped at the only house I saw. Here I was — torn jeans, long hair, and bearded. I asked a flat-topped Marine-type guy if he knew of any places for sale or rent. He looked at me hard — almost through me.

We talked a while and he replied, "Maybe this place is for sale." Silver Falls once again!

More teachers — the hard-core Marine, Pat Paszkiewicz, and his wonderful wife, Sally, taught us how to survive in the country: responsibility and how to use our hands and heads at the same time. We have been friends ever since.

Well, we did our thing — planted trees, pruned berries, and did lots of farm work. We split logs for our shake roof and built a stone fireplace and a log sauna.

Several years later, a message from Billy Kolber. Actually, it wasn't a phone call — we didn't have a phone, but I did receive an overnight mailgram which really impressed the local mailman.

It's time to come back, new company, new designs, new money. Major temptation. Billy insisted, and two days later he arrived late at night and deep in the woods.

Plaid suit, plaid high-heeled shoes, and us — Oregon 1975. It was the first and possibly last time Billy was speechless. Still he managed to bring in his sample case of jeans and jackets adorned with tigers and dragons.

We put him to bed. The next morning over breakfast: *"Anything you want!"* The '52 Jeep, five miles to the store, plaid suit in a phone booth in the forest. Iron will becomes jello. I'm hired!

Taiwan to design a line — Oregon to plant a garden. Hong Kong for business — home for the harvest. Several years of this and serious schizophrenia was setting in. Oregon had beards and funk and family, and the East Coast had 8:00 p.m. meetings, 9:00 p.m. tension, and 10:00 p.m. indigestion. There had to be a better way.

THE EARLY PIECES

One day while stumbling through the woods, Sharon and I came across a freshly logged area. We found these odd-looking "blobs" of wood, which we later discovered were vine maple burls. They had been uprooted when the roads were made. These were small burls, perhaps six to 10 inches in diameter.

We took some home, where we had a rusty all-in-one machine that had been left at the place when we bought it. The table saw walked all over the floor when we turned it on. Its dull blade was enough to cut the burls, and we couldn't believe the beautiful wood. We had never seen wood such as this. The machine also had a lathe, so I clamped on a burl, took my 3/4" carpenter's chisel out, and started to work the wood.

My friend, Russell Swider, schooled as a chemist, but at this time a blacksmith, liked what I was doing during 1979. He persuaded me to buy a bandsaw. We followed ads in the newspapers until we found a 36" saw. When I first stood next to this machine, with its steel blade spinning faster than the speed of light, I was terrified!

Russ had been demonstrating his work at the Oregon State Fair's Craft Courtyard. Started by Judy and Clyde Mullins, this was one of the earliest venues for craftwork in Oregon. Russ decided I should be showing and demonstrating my work. I thought he was kidding because I didn't have any idea what I was doing, and I certainly didn't have the skills to demonstrate woodworking.

My brother Chuck, Sharon, and I joined together and worked all summer to make some boxes, coffee tables, turned pieces, and a chair. We knew little about woodworking or machinery, so we literally hand-sanded each piece and glued the boxes together with a couple of inexpensive C-clamps.

We use mostly Oregon woods. The special pieces we use have grown with the pressures of time and climate; the figurations are a record of the life of the tree.

In August of 1979, we hauled the bandsaw, now painted bright blue, out of the garage and onto our Mazda pickup. Off to the State Fair we went. That little pickup, with the bandsaw standing in the back, surrounded by a whole woodshop, was quite the site driving through town.

In just two days we had sold about everything that we had made that summer — three people working all summer for about $30 a week. With nine days at the Fair to go, we decided we'd better learn how to make these boxes. We rushed to the hardware store, bought more C-clamps and our first belt sander.

"Silver Splinter" was born.

Later in 1979, on a trip to the East Coast, we went to see the Nakashima Showroom. Wow! What a place — such serenity and peacefulness. We even got to exchange a few pleasantries with the Master himself. When Sharon and I got back into our rented car, I was — although embarrassed to even think it — taken by the feeling of Nakashima's work, and that maybe it somehow related to what we were doing.

Later I called him to ask if I could show him our work. He must have gotten many of these types of calls, but he finally consented. I was to bring a "few" pieces to show him that next Saturday when the showroom was open.

When I arrived, excited and nervous — he had that effect on people — I found I had no appointment. No one there had heard of me nor knew I was coming. I waited, and when he came out of his house, the venerable Master in his kimono-style jacket, I jumped out of the bushes and asked again if I could show him my pieces. He consented to look at a couple, so I brought a whole carton into his showroom. I placed them at the entrance and spread them out so that everyone coming into the showroom had to walk over them to enter.

After a while he came over and spent a lot of time talking to us and looking over our boxes. Finally, he asked the prices. Astounded, I asked if he wanted to buy one as a gift. He replied that his intentions were to resell them in his studio.

The great beauty of nature's jewels — gold, silver, diamonds, and pearls — is hidden at the beginning in their rough state.

So it is with the wood we work — the pearls of the forest. Our object is to take this wood with all of its history; to learn its ways and make it into things of natural beauty — functionally organic.

Oregon had beards
and funk and family,
and the East Coast had
8:00 p.m. meetings,
9:00 p.m. tension, and
10:00 p.m. indigestion.
There had to be
a better way.

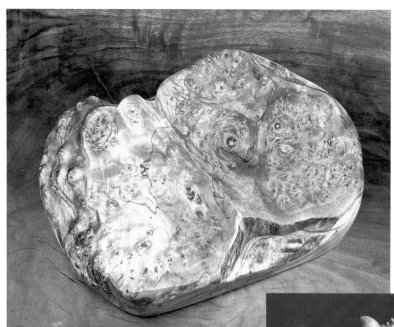

1979-1981

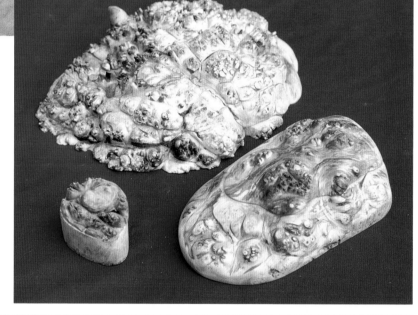

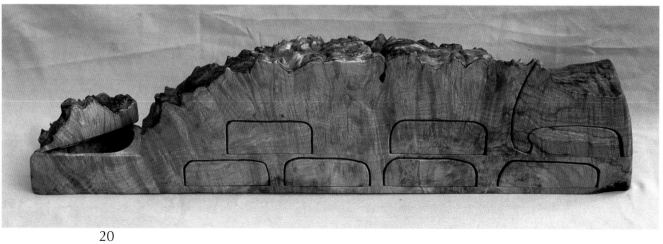

20

1982-1984

1987

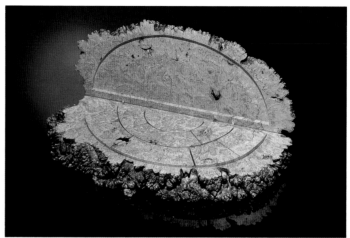

Mañana Time, 1987

Burl Slab Wall Cabinet, 1987

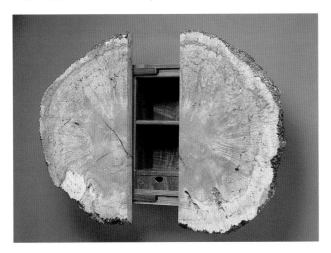

1988

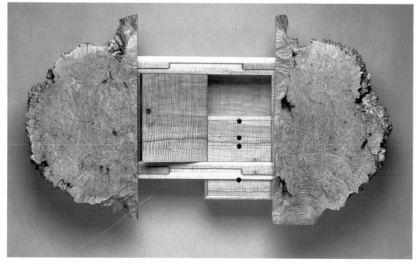

Burl Slab Wall Cabinet, 1988

24

Manana Time and Nesting Boxes, 1989

READING THE WOOD

There are at least two ways of thinking about reading the wood. The first way is to develop an idea or design. The second, or opposite approach, is to just go out and cut some wood! Stand at the bandsaw and see what happens.

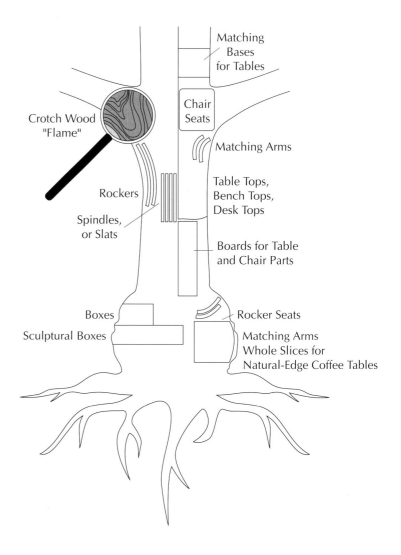

The selection of the parts and of the tree to be used for a project is critical. There must be a joining of rhythms — the start of an interactive process. Each board, and each tree, like man — an individual. Each tree — even each species of tree — has strong grain patterns, wonderful color, or sometimes mellow and simple details.

The world seems to have much trouble with this concept — dealing with these differences of thought, of belief, of color. Perhaps there is a lesson here in this simple material.

Possibly, discovering that each board is perfect and has a perfect use, just as each individual has their own personality — their unique quality, is like stumbling on a point of truth.

I had thought that objects exist in the wood, but it's only recently that I have begun to understand the depth of this process.

I begin with whole trees or huge burls — up to 5,000 pounds each. We mill these with an eye toward their ultimate use, but don't actually know what that might be. The wood is air-dried in the barns for a minimum of one year — some have been stored for 15 years now, still waiting.

After air-drying, we kiln-dry a large group of slabs and chunks for about one month. We then plane off the outside layer to reveal the grain. At this point, I separate the pieces into general categories: furniture, mirrors, dovetail work, sculptural work, and boxes.

I stand pieces up all over the shop, the barn, and the garage — any place I can look at them as I pass by each day.

The concept of generating an idea or design first, is more difficult for me. If there is a commission for a special box or table, I must go through a mountain of wood to find the perfect piece. Often, the box or table must relate to a special site or function.

Nakashima said that each tree and each part of the tree has an ultimate purpose. I also believe this to be true and have fashioned my work to reflect that thought.

I sketch out the project, usually quite crudely because I know I can't copy the sketch exactly. The wood must dictate the piece.

If I don't "read the wood," change from my sketch as I work, the piece simply will not succeed.

This process sometimes happens immediately, and sometimes it takes years.

There is wood on my workbench that has been there for five or six years now.

The second approach could be called "backward thinking." This is easier for me, as I've been accused of this type of thinking many times throughout my life.

Line up a group of boards or chunks of wood, and if their individuality tells you something, start to feel their presence and see their history. Feed on this and experiment!

I cannot tell you how this process works. Periodically, and in a totally random fashion, I'll start to draw on these chunks of wood — sometimes part of an idea, other times a complete thought. None of this is sketched on paper because each piece of wood is so different and has its own character. At times I want to work and try to force designs. The work is then tedious.

Then there are days when I can't stop! I draw and cut for hours, almost in a delirious state. Things just happen. The pieces go together as if willed to do so. When the rhythms flow together, it is sometimes magical!

Feel the shape, size, texture, and grain. This may dictate a function or a scene or an object. When I work at the saw, I aim to keep my mind open to the wood and, at the same time, focused on its possibilities.

While I was designing clothing, one of the lessons constantly repeated was to eliminate the preconceived notions.

Therefore, I study the wood. As I set each piece on the saw, I clean it off, cut an edge, and strive for its ultimate use. Some pieces may become simple hand mirrors with extravagant grain flowing through the handle or perhaps boxes in an infinite variety of shapes. Much of the work we do uses live-edged wood, or the natural configuration of the wood. It is somewhat confined in a geometric shape, but its extravagance cannot be totally contained within the form.

Many times the wood is put aside, waiting for its appropriate use. I have hundreds of pieces lying around. I can't count how many times I moved those giant slabs before their essence and mine had a meeting. Recently, I did a sculptural box from a tree I chainsaw-milled 15 years ago.

There are no scientific formulas for "reading the wood." It is a feeling. It is an art.

Aztecco

Usually, my best work is the easiest, and it takes the least amount of time and effort.

I still enjoy the process — a new object, a new shape for a box. A Mayan vision evolves, or perhaps seeing the trees leaning over each other in the forest suggests some architectural form.

29

PART TWO

The Tree — A Material of Expression

MAPLE BURL

We use mostly Oregon woods. The special pieces we use have grown with the pressures of time and climate. The figurations are a record of the life of the tree.

Primarily, we use Oregon big leaf maple burl, said to occur on one tree in one thousand. Their leaves resemble an open hand and can measure up to 12 inches in diameter. The idea of using burls is very different than using wood from the trunk of a tree. Burls don't grow the same and so there are no straight or wavy grains. Instead, they have an almost circular pattern of figure.

When using burls, you don't use boards. Instead, you start with "chunks" or "slabs."

As a boy, I don't remember any trees.

END OF 13 WEEKS: Mike is becoming lazy. He has the ability to do his work better but seems to dream a great deal. He needs extra help in numbers and spelling.

END OF SECOND TERM: Mike still dreams. May those dreams come true! He is a most willing and helpful child.

Assigned to Grade 2A (room 207) September 9 19 49

PERIOD	SIGNATURE OF PARENT OR GUARDIAN
7 Weeks	Frances Elkan
13 Weeks	Frances Elkan
First Term	Frances Elkan
7 Weeks	Frances Elkan
13 Weeks	Frances Elkan

I've noticed through the years that being in the trees, and touching them, gives me energy. There's a certain reverence for natural sites which are in their ancient and original state.

This leads to a difficult transition in trying to tell you about having respect for the trees, and then cutting them down.

The two actions can contradict each other.

There is always a shudder of anticipation when I see a tree to be cut; most times I'd rather see it standing. Then, I'm working the wood and it's just flowing. The work, almost without thought, is chalked onto the wood, like a flowing creek. The most satisfying pieces happen this way.

Burl is a cluster of dormant buds. These buds are what create the figure called bird's-eye. Burls can occur on the base of a tree, just above the root system, or sometimes on the trunk. When the entire trunk has many of these burls, it is called a cluster log or cluster tree. Loggers refer to the burls below as "stump burls."

I have never read a definite explanation about what causes the tree to burl. The trees appear to be healthy and seem to live as long as trees without burls. One oddity is, when a tree is cut, if one or more burls are left in the ground, new trees will grow.

Burls form on many different kinds of trees, but with little apparent formula. Sometimes in a group of maples, all will have burls or none will. It is a mystery. In the area of our home, we have many maple trees, but none have burls.

I have seen them on old and damaged trees and on young trees only four to six inches in diameter — sometimes with a two- to three-foot-diameter burl at the base. I have seen burls as large as a small car and as small as a baseball.

The figuring can take on many different patterns. What is inside can be read from the outside when the bark is removed. The "bumps" are sometimes tight and pointy and as sharp as berry stickers, and other times they are quite smooth.

When I started using burls, they were mostly known as waste wood. There were a few people using them for wall clocks and tabletops and some drawer-type boxes done in redwood. Most maple trees were chipped for paper. Maple trees can be quite fascinating. They contain patterns that are unusual. These can occur on almost any species of tree. Some of these figurings are called curlywood, fiddleback (commonly used for musical instruments such as guitars), and marbled wood.

Back in 1979, I went to a local lumberyard, which had pallets of burl stuck in the back of the store behind a loading dock. One day, while snooping around, I found them. It was like stumbling onto a buried treasure. Over a period of several months, I acquired about 30 of these pallets of burls. I paid about $50 a pallet, but I had to sort through each pile and pull out the perfect clock faces. These were the pieces which had a natural burl all around the edges and the only ones the store could regularly sell.

My interest was in the box material, and it could have one cut side. Actually, this was my introduction to "reading the wood" and using it appropriately.

Unlike milling wood from the trunk of a tree to get uniform boards, here every cut produces a different-size piece with different grain patterns, voids, and shapes.

After I had used the best pieces for boxes, I still had a mountain of wood to deal with. Other possible projects suddenly became apparent — hand mirrors, different shapes for boxes, a chair seat, a head board. Wow! The more I worked with the wood, the more I saw.

We work this material as an instrument, to fashion useful objects, possibly if so willed a thing of beauty — in any case a joining of the rhythms of nature to fulfill its destiny and ours.

— George Nakashima

All the pieces we make are from solid wood. Each stick is looked at and a decision is made — no board or chunk is used haphazardly.

The grain, shape, size, and innate feeling must relate to the function of the piece to be made; not just knowledge of wood, but a feeling that all of nature is repeating itself uniquely.

Each piece — the only one of its kind.

Combination clock and dovetailed stamp dispenser

This was the beginning of what I call "one-of-a-kind" production. Each piece — the only one of its kind.

Over the years this developed into a line of work — small and more production-oriented, furniture, and sculptural pieces — each in keeping with the concept of using the wood for its optimum purpose.

Over time, it grew, as the burled trees grow. No apparent formula, but instead, a flow of ideas and purpose to present the wood; virtually setting the wood on a pedestal and keeping its continuity.

Dovetail boxes

Oval mirror boxes

Hand mirrors

BURL COLLECTORS

Maple burl comes from areas which have either been clear-cut or from private wood lots. Maples are generally taken to be chipped for the paper industry.

The burl cutters, who are specialists, will acquire a permit to enter these areas and take any burls left before the area is torched. The controlled fires are to burn off the small brush and plants, and feed the soil for newly planted monoculture.

Clear-cuts are probably the most depressing places I've ever seen, and unfortunately, I've seen more than my share.

As woodworkers, using natural resources, we have a responsibility.

In less time than it takes to read a chapter in this book, possibly hundreds of animal and plant species will disappear from the Earth forever.

Here in the northwest, about 90 percent of our ancient forests which once blanketed our land are now gone. Someday future generations might walk through a remaining splendid cathedral of ancient trees and will wonder how it could have been that the destruction of such a magnificent and timeless resource continued for so long.

The burled maples will usually grow again if any part of the burl is left in the ground. They might also regenerate if the area is not sprayed to kill off the competing broadleaf plants.

Fox glove, fireweed, and other plants would appear in the clearings. Alder trees, which are leguminous and feed the soil nitrogen, come and go as the more hearty fir trees set their roots. This forms a more natural and mixed forest which is generally healthier for all living things.

The removal of the burls is incredibly tedious and backbreaking work. Burls often weigh 2,000 to 5,000 pounds each, and are generally attached to the root system. Cutting through dirt and rocks, it is not uncommon for a chainsaw chain to be used up rapidly.

I've heard stories of burls being carried out of the woods for a quarter mile or more because they were near creeks or in ravines and were not accessible by machinery.

Years ago, when an area was clear-cut, large seed trees were left to propagate in a natural fashion. This method, although it took longer, allowed for a more natural transition. No one knows the entire story, but either method may not work.

Most of the woods I have used since I began working are secondary-use woods. Much of this decision has to do with my ecological stance. I have found many beautiful woods that are not commonly used. It's a good feeling to use a wood which normally might be burned or chipped or left to rot.

When I started doing this work, I went everywhere to find wood, and many times I still do. I have oftentimes found burls in barns, sheds, basements, and attics, where people have saved wood for many years. It sounds strange, but some people actually do this!

I've found wood 40 to 50 years old through ads in local papers and by word-of-mouth. I've scavenged the lumberyards in many cases, looking through the so-called "junk wood" stashed behind and under piles of dust.

RAINFOREST WOODS

THE SMART WOOD PROGRAM:
Promoting Environmental Wood Products by Kate Heaton

Smart Wood is a program of the Rainforest Alliance, which was founded in 1986, to conserve tropical forests. Smart Wood is the oldest and largest independent forestry certification program. The goal is to identify and promote well-managed "sources" of timber that do not destroy forests. The program originated in the tropics and now operates in all forest types. Smart Wood assessments are based on guidelines with criteria to evaluate environmental impacts, sustainable timber production, and social impacts. Michael Elkan was the first craftsman to sign up for this program.

A decision to use a tropical timber species should be based more on the type of operation that supplies it than on the species being used. If an operation is well-managed, it should make little difference which species are harvested, although if a species is considered rare, threatened, endangered, vulnerable, or overharvested, an effort should be made to use less vulnerable species.

Consumers will not know how wood is harvested unless they ask if the source is recognized or certified as "well-managed." Today the demand for certified wood products is greater than the supply. Fortunately, consumers of wood products can help assure that the supply will grow in the future by using their buying power to demonstrate that there is market demand for such products.

The Rainforest Alliance does not advocate timber boycotts. Although valuable in drawing attention to issues, they do not improve management, they transfer problems elsewhere, and they can devalue the forest resource. Being able to see that forests have value, increases the chance that they will be managed, instead of cleared for pasture or agriculture. This is especially true in parts of the tropics where there is pressure on the land to yield an economic return, as is often the case due to population growth. From an economic standpoint, many times it appears that clearing forests is favorable, but in reality, good forest management can yield far better economic results while keeping the forests standing. Thus, timber production, if done sustainably, can be used as a tool to help save forests.

Sustainable forestry practices can reduce harvesting impacts on surrounding forests by 50 percent and assure continued future supplies of timber and habitat because harvest levels do not exceed what the forest can regenerate. Furthermore, sustainable forestry practices combat overharvesting of popular species by encouraging the controlled use of new lesser known species.

The potential sustainability of forestry should not, however, be used as a blanket excuse for logging in all areas. Many areas should not be disturbed at all. There are many remote, pristine areas with little population pressure that should remain untouched.

In the book, *Islands of Fire, Islands of Spice"* by Richard Bangs and Christian Kallen, they say a book held at arms length is a bit like an Indonesian Rainforest. When viewed from the air, with a sweep of the eye, both appear orderly, orchestrated, elegant — perhaps the work of a single artist. There is little evidence of the chaos beneath the canopy, of the great tangle of organisms, their complex interrelationships, and the monumental amount of energy involved in creating the complicated, but deceptively simple looking whole.

I have coded each wood with either "BS" for bandsaw work or "RW" for router work. This is based solely on how I am using the wood and my experiences, but I would urge the woodworker to try new approaches.

CHAKTEKOK (RW)

Chaktekok is from the Yucatan in Mexico. This is from a cooperative sponsored by the Rainforest Alliance. This wood, and several others, are logged from a rainforest and are certified and checked periodically for logging practices which hopefully will result in a sustainable yield.

The chaktekok has a fabulous red color with dark highlights and sometimes a curly lighter figure. The color is sensational and it works beautifully. The 4/4 stock is of excellent quality. The 8/4 is difficult to dry and often needs a lot of extra time in the shop to settle out. Beware not to buy these boards with the heart in the board as they will crack. It finishes very well.

CHECHEN (RW)

Chechen is also from the Yucatan. It is very dense and can vary in color and pattern significantly. It is basically brown with dark lines, but sometimes it has wonderful figuring and color variations from cream to black. It is easily worked, but it is slow to drill. It takes a beautiful finish, much like rosewoods.

GRANADILLO (RW)

Granadillo is also from the Yucatan and other areas of Mexico. This wood is not necessarily a rainforest wood. I only use certified granadillo. It also has many variations, from a soupy red color to deep purple with black highlights and is very dense. It works similar to chechen and finishes well.

SECONDARY-USE WOODS

GILMER WOOD COMPANY by Myles Gilmer

Scarcity of world resources, depletion of the tropical rainforests, environmentalist calls to limit solid-wood construction — these and other concerns give today's woodworkers cause for concern. In the last few years, timber dealers and importers have seen supplies of once common woods become depleted or soar in price. These include genuine mahogany, Burma teak, Indian rosewood, bird's-eye maple, and the ebonies. The future will probably see the supplies of many other species decline as well. Consequently, we have been experimenting for years with secondary, or less-utilized, timbers, plantation species, and improving wood-recovery rates. There are far more wood mass and diverse wood species available today than there were just 10 to 20 years ago. Today's professional or serious woodworking hobbyist has a cornucopia of woods available to him or her.

More sophisticated methods of harvest, i.e., sustained-yield / low-impact removal, have given us the opportunity to play around with some of these species and learn their unique characteristics. Timber dealers are increasingly trying these newly introduced species, even though, being untested, they are sometimes a tough sell to consumers. It is up to these merchants to educate their customers to the unique qualities of these species.

As a timber dealer, I am always willing to try new species so as to determine their pluses and minuses. Woodworkers can use species once considered as pests and often burned in loggers' slash piles. Woods such as the maples have almost always been rejected because of dark hearts or mineral streaks or stains, but these natural discolorations are oftentimes quite beautiful and can be used as an eye-catching asset to a piece of furniture or jewelry box. Pacific yew, found as an understory species in northwest Douglas fir forests and usually discarded, is a beautiful furniture and accessory wood and also highly valued by builders of archery bows. I think it is also paramount to try and get as much yield as possible out of a tree, and I develop programs to cut squares and small billets for box-makers, musical instrument makers, furniture manufacturers, etc. I offer incentives to woodworkers who try and use smaller pieces of wood. When I contract with a mill to supply me with lumber, I, of course, am interested in nice wide, long, clear boards, but I also order small blocks and squares, some as small as 1" x 1" x 4", so as to utilize more of the resource. I encourage customers to use the waste wood from other projects — the ultimate object is to resource close to 100 percent of the total biomass of a tree.

When I first got into the wood import business in the 1970s, there were approximately 600 commercial species of hardwoods

I am reminded of some of my favorite spots, at Opal Creek Ancient Forest Area. There on the path is a fir tree over 1,000 years old. Awesome. Just to stand under it sends shivers up the spine. Also, in this area there are 1,000 year old cedars, walking through this is almost surreal.

available. In the 1990s, this number has doubled because of the interest in maintaining the world's forests. We are fortunate that today there are timber dealers, importers, and mills that are providing an entire new host of species for the woodworker.

Dovetail bookends

HOLLY (RW)

Holly is white, white, white. This is one of my favorite woods and works great. I've heard that these small trees must be cut down, milled, and vacuum-dried within three days to prevent the wood from staining. If allowed to sit, the wood turns a funny shade of blue. I finish holly with wax only.

KOA (RW)

Koa is from Hawaii. It works wonderfully and can have some of the most sensational curl and figure. The luscious lustre is unbeatable, but unfortunately, koa is getting hard to find. Koa takes on an excellent finish.

LACEWOOD (RW)

Lacewood comes from Brazil. This wood's main feature is the flake pattern, from very delicate to almost 1/2"-diameter flakes. Lacewood works and finishes well.

PEROBA ROSA (RW)

Peroba Rosa has a wonderful pink color sometimes interspersed with yellow. I call it "Brazilian Pinkwood" and I originally found this wood in pallets. It works good and finishes well.

REDWOOD BURL (RW, BS)

The redwoods are the most majestic trees I've ever seen. The story of this noble tree could fill the pages of an entire book. Much of this has been decimated, but there are still people pulling it out of the rivers and canyons where roots and stumps were dumped when they cleared land many years ago. The wood we get is generally very old and very rare. Sometimes redwood burl is soft and fragile. The figuring can be wonderfully tight lacy burl to curly wood. You have to fit the wood perfectly to the project because it can be tricky to work and finish. It requires some experimenting.

SYCAMORE (RW)

Sycamore, when quarter sawn, has a very delicate flake pattern in dark and light honey colors. Traditionally, this wood was used inside cabinet work and even upholstered furniture and drawers. It is a beautiful wood, but extremely delicate. It works well and finishes nicely.

Each box we make is from a single piece of extraordinary wood. It is the idea and the goal. The wood is the most important element, one-of-a-kind, because we cannot make two alike.

Listed are additional woods I've worked that I would consider "odd" woods.

ALDER (RW, BS)

Alder is softer and lighter than maple. I only use alder when I spalt it. It is a little tricky because it rots rapidly, but it is quite beautiful when you have been successful with the spalting process.

BOX ELDER BURL (RW, BS)

Box elder is creamy white, but turns yellow. It is not my favorite burl because of the color change and it usually has lots of bark pockets. When it has good spalting with bright red, it is quite fantastic. Always finish with wax only.

BUCKEYE BURL (RW, BS)

Buckeye has splotchy blue and white burls and is in the chestnut family. It is beautiful, but usually has lots of dirt and is very soft. It can make spectacular pieces and finishes pretty well. I finish with wax only. Oils will turn the wood yellow.

COCONUT PALM (RW)

Coconut palm is a red palm and is fabulous looking. It takes a great finish, but requires some experimenting. It also splinters easily. At this time, there is no cure for the blight which is decimating palm trees around the world.

ELM BURL (RW, BS)

Elm burl is hard, dense, and can have some of the tightest bird's-eyes I've ever seen. I'm still experimenting with this wood and I air-dry elm burl for at least one year. It needs a lot of time to mellow, but it is worth the wait! It has great color, a kind of reddish orange, and works very well. It finishes great.

FRUITWOODS (RW)

Fruitwoods would include peach, plum, apple, pear, and cherry. All of these woods, except apple, are wonderful. The color and working properties are good, but because the trees are usually small, you must do small projects. Warping can be a problem, so the wood needs to be air-dried for a long time.

MYRTLEWOOD (RW, BS)

Myrtlewood works very well and finishes well. The colors can be creamy with black highlights or kind of greenish. The natural outside is not usually exciting enough for me, but being very selective you can find some exciting pieces.

WHITE OAK (RW)

White oak is from the northwest. It is oak — the classic wood.

I keep a gigantic inventory of wood on hand at all times. It is in many different states of drying and preparation. This is in keeping with my philosophy of reading the wood, and possibly because I'm somewhat of a wood junkie, but mostly it's there because of how we make our choices.

Each stick is looked at and a decision is made. No board or chunk is used haphazardly. Having a large selection to choose from has several advantages.

Making a variety of pieces, as we do, it is possible to make the appropriate choices for each project. This limits the amount of compromising.

By having lots of wood to look at, often I get new ideas, which the wood itself projects. As I pass by a stack, potential uses may suggest themselves.

In a very practical manner, I can dry the wood in a slower fashion — air drying for a minimum of one year. This allows the wood to mellow, it feels better in the working, and I experience much fewer problems with warping.

By looking at and handling thousands of pieces of wood, I've discovered it's not all the same — it's not like metal, plastic, or clay. I look at each one and make a decision on its use. Each piece is individual and possibly has an ultimate purpose.

My friend, Clyde Aspenwall, loved collecting wood, and, when I met him in about 1979, he had set up a mill on his farm and was cutting walnut trees.

He would sell musical-instrument wood and gun blanks. It seemed he always had the most beautiful walnut. Every tree was a winner, unlike the wood I saw at the lumberyards, where much of it looked almost colorless in comparison.

Clyde had a theory. He left the trees out in the fields for at least a year or two to mellow out. The tannon and the juices would meld together and colors would become richer. I have no scientific evidence for this, but I still like to do the same and I've seen the difference.

Using this concept, some of the natural edges are lost. Bugs will eat the sap wood, but what is left is even more delicious. This can depend on which tree is used. For instance, maple may be left out for three months, more or less. It starts to spalt almost immediately, and if let go too long, it will rot. Often, I have left wood out to purposely spalt — maple and alder are excellent choices for this. Time, different climatic conditions, and the soil all make a difference.

Of course, there are lots of woods I've still not used and I am always looking for new ones.

Many of the miraculous properties of trees and their ecosystem haven't been discovered yet. It might be said that not only do we not have the answers to the many complex questions, but we may not know the correct questions.

The cycles of nature — droughts, wind, fire, and rain — our living history, is recorded in the ancient trees which typically begin exhibiting old-growth characteristics at 200 years.

PART THREE

The Tree
in Transition

The traditions of woodworking are ancient. The first wheel and sleds for moving objects may have been wood — possibly our first tools. In every ancient culture, there were temple builders and possibly box-makers using wood. As the Native Americans might say: We must stand on the shoulders of those before us, follow the light of their knowledge and wisdom — maybe go a step further.

TOOLS OF THE TRADE

For the type of work I do, the bandsaw is the most crucial tool. I don't know if the objects led to the saw or the saw to the objects, but of all the tools possible for carving wood, this feels the most comfortable.

My first saw was a 36" and was made by a machinist named Larry Sterling. It had steamed oak wheels and a fabricated metal body and table, with a 1/4" blade it could cut a 3/4"-diameter plug in 3" solid oak.

I used this saw for six or seven years, when a friend told me he knew of a saw in San Francisco that was for sale for $900. It was an old "Oliver" built in 1942 and shipped to Hughes Aircraft. Immediately, I called and bought the saw. It had bits of plywood dust inside when it arrived. I like to believe it worked on the "spruce goose" which was in production at that time.

I tuned the saw, new guides, truing and balancing the wheels, new tires, and a phase converter. Here in the Oregon woods, we have no three-phase electric.

I had a fence specially made. It was designed in collaboration with the Biesemeyer Company. They were great about working out this project. The fence in this type work is indispensable; it is moved on virtually every cut and must be accurate, easy, and dependable.

I have a third bandsaw, which is used for smaller cuts, carving the insides of boxes and finer sculptural work. This 20" Italian saw has never been as satisfying to work with as the Oliver.

There are several important criteria for a bandsaw in our type of work — flexibility is foremost. I use the big saw for chunking burls, sometimes up to 200 pounds and 21 inches tall. This work requires a heavy tool with a powerful motor, set on a solid foundation.

The wheels must be aligned and balanced, and the tires crowned. The guides should be easy to adjust. The saw must be quiet — the noise can kill you. One of the details manufacturers often miss is a convenient way to raise and lower the guides. You should be able to do this from the front of the saw.

When working with a minimum of space between the guides and the wood, the cut is smoother, straighter, and, in turn, easier to handle. I use only a 1/2" blade of .025 thickness. This is quite unusual for such a large saw blade length of 18 feet 9 inches. The thinness of the kerf, or cut, is critical to our work. It is obvious everything matches better when the least amount of wood is removed.

On the small saw, we use a 1/4" blade of .025 thickness. These are all standard four tooth-skip flexible back blades.

I received my worst injury on a table saw and they still scare me. I guess I've never learned to use it correctly. However, considering how a tree grows, and how we use the wood, the ability to cut along grain lines, in and around figuring, makes sense.

A table saw cuts straight lines and it may dictate how a board is to be cut.

The complex character of the wood is perfect for the versatility of the bandsaw. Even on furniture projects, it is our first choice for a cutting tool.

Of course, we use many other tools, but I thought the bandsaw deserved special mention.

This is not an example of mechanics or exceptional joinery, but instead, a somewhat tenacious and kind of innate desire of expression. I think that is what makes each piece a blend of man and nature which is sometimes magical.

WORK IN PROGRESS

Very few American woodworkers have experienced a true apprenticeship. In Japan or Europe, apprentices work in shops for years before being allowed to touch a chisel or saw. We usually learn the craft from reading — and, most importantly, from doing. And, as my friend Norman says, the "How-To" book is still being written.

In this learning process, I have come to believe more is better. By that I mean, the more you repeat a project or piece, the more you understand the wood and the processes of working wood.

In my case, wanting to earn my living working wood led me to doing what I call one-of-a-kind production. This is my apprenticeship.

For starting out in this field, I would advise you on the many benefits of production. I love things that work well, are minimalist, and almost perfect in their function. The aspect of repetitiveness unveils how the wood moves and reacts to humidity, temperature, or sunlight. It recommends which tools will cut or sand the best. Eventually, this interactive process might lead to new discoveries, techniques, or designs — maybe simplifying a process or an object.

If you take a board and cut a hundred circles for mirrors — it's production as we know it. If you take the same board, and "read the wood", the possibilities are endless.

Keeper Boxes:
Step-by-Step

I call the basic bandsawn box a "keeper." This is because the part that holds the lift-off lid onto the body keeps it in place. Most any wood is suitable, and the shapes and sizes are endless. The only requirement: trying! The keeper shown is called the "camel-back."

1

After blocking out a piece of wood, I cut a curved lid.

2

Shown in parts:
A — Lid
B — Body
C — Bottom
D — Keeper (the part
       removed from
       the body)

3

Mark out the interior shape. The corners are shown square, but will be rounded off when cut.

4

Cutting in progress.
The top is marked
with a "K" for keeper.
This will have
glue applied later.

The inside piece will
be the keeper.

5

Using a stiff piece of glossy paper (postcard) with glue on it, spread the glue. Take care not to get glue inside the box when clamped.

6

Clamp the side. Glue can squeeze to the outside to show full contact.

7

While applying glue to the keeper, stay away from the edges. The "K" is disc sanded, along with the bottom of the lid, for a perfect fit with no gaps showing.

8

Set the lid and the body upside down. Align the keeper piece with the lid.

9

Carefully lift off the body and hold the keeper and the lid together for about 20 seconds, or until the glue is tacky and won't move. The keeper is done.

10

After the glue has dried completely, cut off the excess wood to form the lid and the keeper. For gluing on the bottom, refer to the Hinged Boxes, Steps 8, 9, and 10, on pages 71 and 72. The box is now ready for sanding, oiling, and waxing.

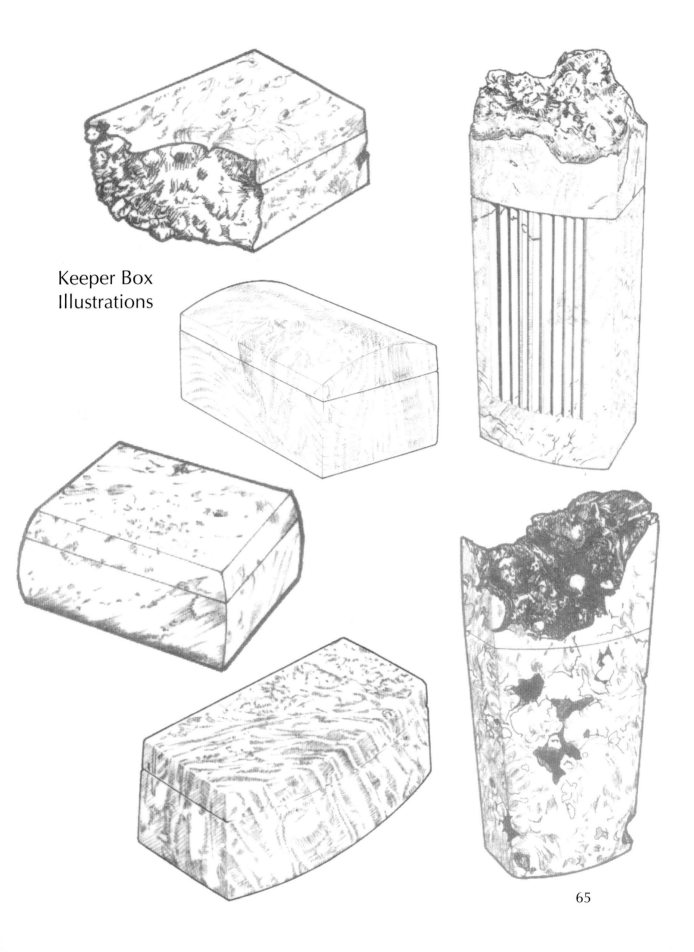

Keeper Box
Illustrations

Hinged Boxes:
Step-by-Step

1

I shaped this box by cutting angled sides and a straight back. The size and shape are not crucial in a functional sense. Only the straight back is needed for the hinges.

2

Cut the lid and the bottom.

Lid — approximately 3/4" to 7/8"

Bottom — approximately 1/4" to 5/16"

3

Mark the interior of the box. Leave 7/8" of an inch on the back for the barrel hinges.

4

In this case,
the box has
stepped corners
and a separate
divided section.

5

Using a 1/4" blade,
cut through the side
and, for now, remove
the interior.

6

Cutting the
pleats, or
stepped
corners.

7

Shape
and cut
the divider.

8

After gluing the cut side, refer to the Keeper Boxes, Steps 5 and 6, on page 62. Apply the glue to the bottom of the body. Do not allow the glue to migrate to the inside since it cannot be cleaned up. Always sand the inside of the bottom to show the wood's figuring, but only the inside. Don't sand the parts to be glued. The pieces will fit best when left in their original state.

9

Clamp the back edge first, but make sure the natural edge will align perfectly.

10

Place the bottom on the body. Lay a piece of good plywood over this (we use a 1"-thick plywood block with a very slight depression in the center). When the clamp is applied to the top center, it pushes the block flat and clamps the whole length equally. Use as many blocks as needed to force the glue to show around all the outer edges. No seams should show. The gluing block is used in lieu of multiple clamps — for a hinged box we might use eight clamps for a seamless fit.

11

Clean up cuts using a 1"-strip sander or by hand sanding.

12

Spreading glue on the bridge, I place it back in its original spot and glue it down using a clamp and block.

13

Disc sand the
bottom of the lid
and the top of the
body to flatten.
Finish-sand, trying
not to change
the shape.

14

Align the hinges
and mark both
the body and
the lid. Drill the
body first, and
use points to
align the holes.
Place the
lid on top
to mark the
drilling spots.
Finally, drill
the lid. We use
either 10 or 12mm
barrel hinges.

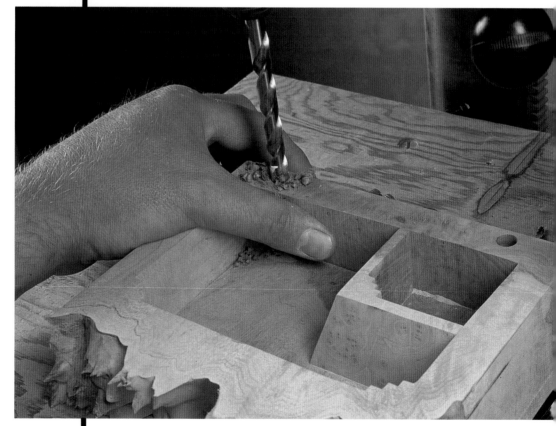

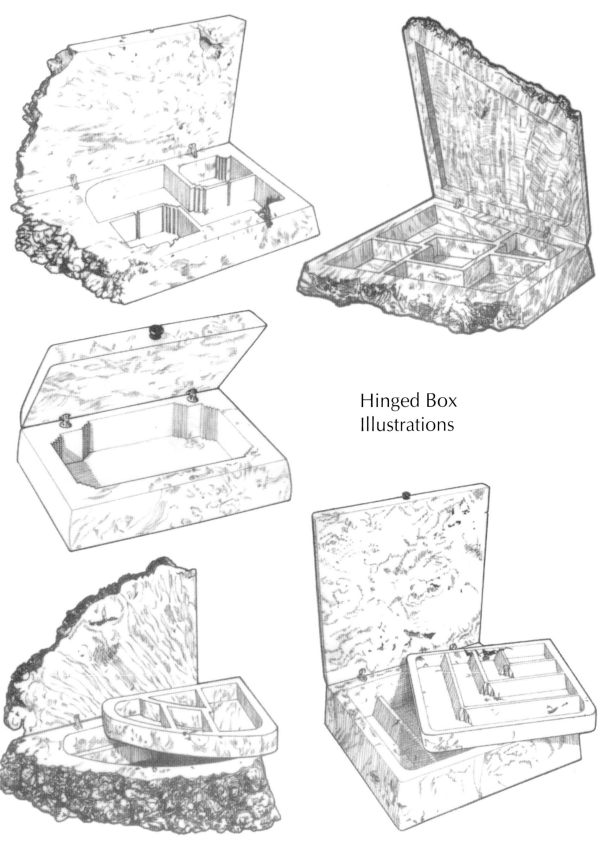

Hinged Box
Illustrations

Sculptural Pieces:
Step-by-Step

1

For this multi-arch design,
I lay the piece out using
a straightedge and a compass.

A — Bottom
B — Arches
C — Bottom for
    Overlapping Arches
D — Overlapping Arches
E — Bottom for Keeper
F — Box Section
G — Lid

77

2

The whole
is then cut
into sections —
parts A through G.

3

Parts A
through G
are shown
sliced from
the burl slab.

4

Mark and cut pleats; then cut out the arches using a 1/4" blade.

5

Cut the overlapping arches, much like carving, using a 1/4" blade.

6

Clean off the burn marks and smooth out the cuts made in Step 5.

7

Parts have been cut and stacked up. Double-check to make sure all wanted cuts have been made. To finish container portion of the sculpture, you must follow all of the steps for making a keeper box on pages 59-64.

8

While applying the glue, be sure to wipe off the edges to assure no glue seeps to the inside or into the pleats. It is okay if glue seeps to the outside because this surface will eventually be sanded.

9

Using clamps, glue all the parts together. This photo shows Part D (overlapping arches) being glued to Part C (bottom for overlapping arches).

10

Finally,
chip off the
bark, anyway
you can being
careful of
your knuckles.

84

Sculptural
Illustrations

KEN ALTMAN

I would like to introduce you to Ken Altman's dovetail box. His work is a wonderful example of using the subtractive art concept.

Ken is probably the finest craftsman I've known, learned from, and worked with. He has a rare blend of technical perfection and the ability to "read the wood" and use it appropriately. He uses a minimalist approach with elegant, yet simple hardware. His delicate touch is apparent in the musical instruments he now makes.

Ken's techniques are perfect for creating projects involving routed work: mirrors, boxes, dovetail works.

Dovetail Boxes:
Step-by-Step

The idea for these dovetail boxes came to me after Michael mentioned a puzzle he had seen. It was a cube, made of two pieces of metal dovetailed together in a seemingly impossible way, with the dovetails showing on the four adjacent sides. The trick is that the two halves of the puzzle are joined together with sliding dovetails running diagonally through the piece. After making one, it occurred to me to route a cavity between the sliding dovetails, making the cube into a box.

1

Router table set up
for machining dovetails.

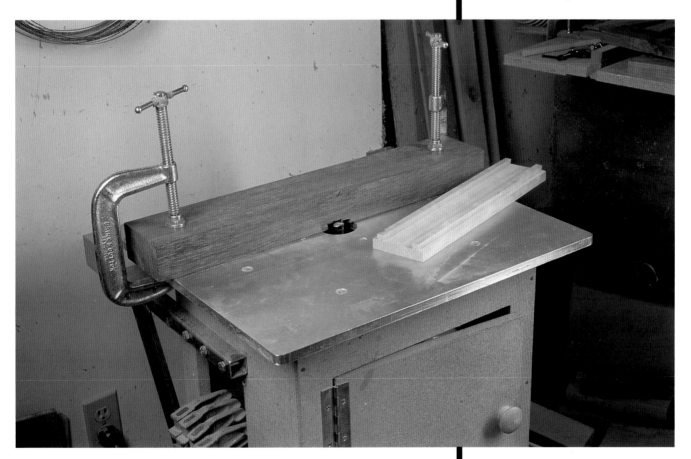

2

Begin with a
dimensioned board
one to two feet long.
After most of the waste
wood is dadoed out
on the table saw, the
dovetails for the bottom
of the boxes are routed.
One dovetail is routed,
the board is turned end
for end, and the other
dovetail is routed.

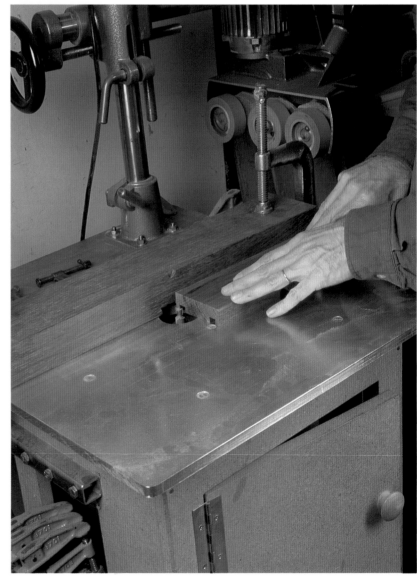

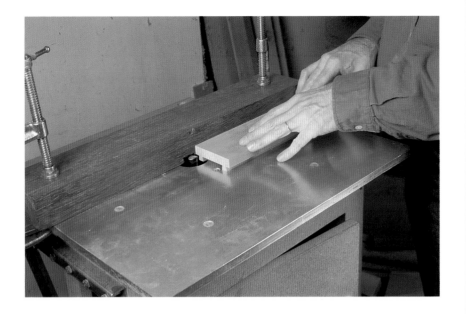

3

Then the outside of the top dovetails are routed. Most of the waste is removed on the table saw. One of the dovetails is routed, the board is turned, and the other side is routed. The width of these dovetails is checked for fit against the dovetails already routed in the box bottoms. The fit of the dovetails can be precisely adjusted by loosening the clamp holding the fence, and gently tapping it toward or away from the cutter.

4

The inside edges of the dovetails in the top are routed. The fit of the dovetails can now be checked with the box bottoms. The dovetails should slide freely, allowing a little room for the wood to expand and contract.

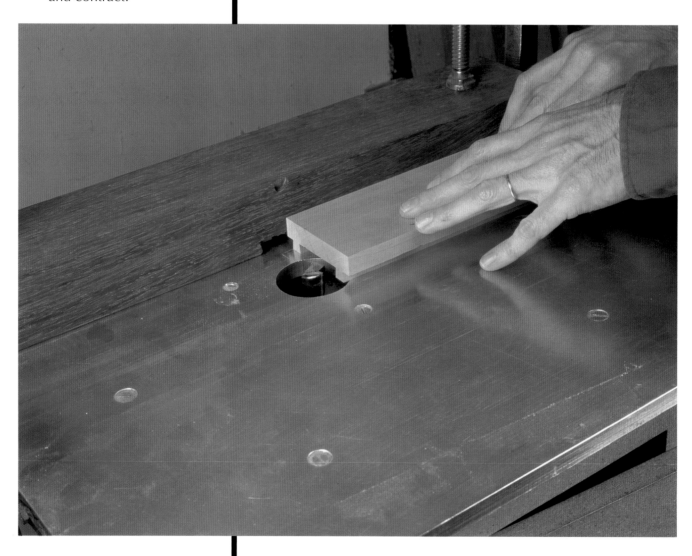

5

With the stock for the top and bottom of the box mated together, the outline is drawn on the top using a template. The outline of the box, whether square or oval, is oriented diagonally on the dovetailed stock.

6

The top and bottom can be tacked together with a small nail, in an area of the stock that will be waste, to keep them from sliding apart as the box is cut out. Cut out the box on the bandsaw, staying slightly outside of the line.

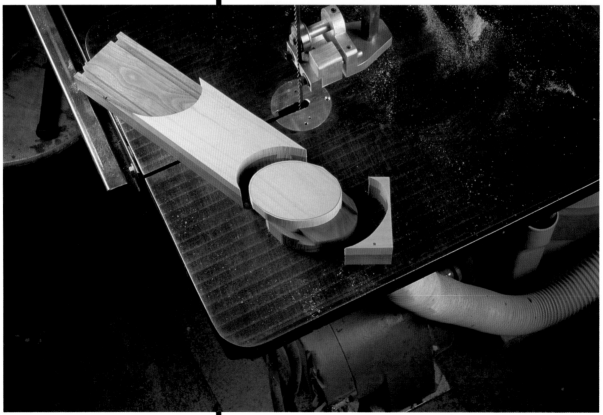

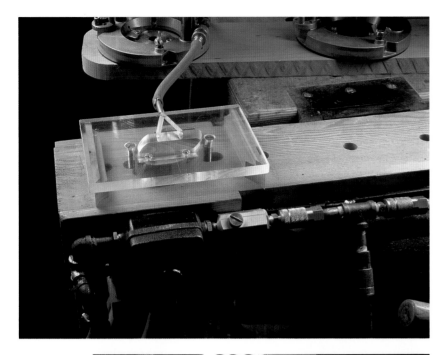

7

The bottom of the box is held under a routing template, made of 1/2" Plexiglas. The set up in this photo uses pneumatic cylinders to apply clamping pressure. Simply securing the template with screws will work as well. The air hose going into the template is to blow the chips out of the recess as it is being routed. The pneumatic cylinders and this air hose are used to make this process more efficient, but are not otherwise necessary.

8

Machine the inside of the box using a router guided by the Plexiglas template with a template guide bushing installed on the router.

9

With the top and bottom of the box clamped together, the half of the box opposite the clamp is sanded to the outline on a stationary belt sander. The clamp is then moved to the sanded side, and the remainder of the outline is sanded.

10

Hidden inside the dovetail, in the lid, is a small brass leaf spring which keeps the tension on the dovetail to keep the lid closed. A keyhole slot cutter is used with this jig on the router table to route the slot for the spring. The stops on either side of the cutter are set to make the slot about 1/2" longer than the spring.

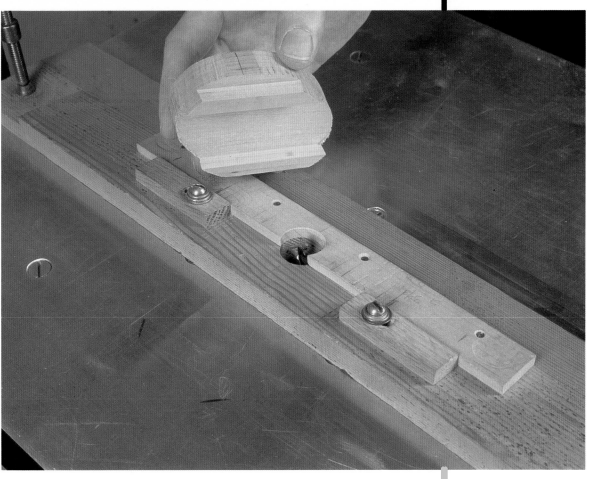

11

Drill the hole for the screw that holds the spring in place. The extended drill bit was made by drilling a hole in the end of a piece of steel rod, then super-gluing the drill bit into this hole.

12

Secure the spring in place with a small wood screw. The box is now ready for fine sanding and finishing.

FINISHING WOODS

Finishing is the soul of our endeavor. Of course, this may be the most time-consuming process. At the studio, we pride ourselves on the finish of our works.

We have spent all this time and energy to lay out the correct figure on the piece and construct or subtract to reveal this object. Now is the time to find the depth of the wood. There is more there than what is on the surface and a fine finish will reveal this.

On small pieces we surface-sand or disc-sand to true the piece and get it flat and level. Any sanding machine will work, depending on the size of the project. Generally #120 grit, relatively course, is best at this stage.

Using a 1/4 or 1/2 sheet palm sander, start with #80 or #100 grit to remove the scratches of the #120 belts. Check by holding at an angle to the light. You may have some swirls, but no scratches are allowed.

Now you are ready for finish sanding. Using #150 grit with the palm sander should take out the swirls. This is not the place for shortcuts.

The piece should start to feel smooth. Using #220 grit removes swirls and scratches and leaves a slightly polished finish. Using #400 grit takes off most of the hairs and polishes the surface. Blow it off with an air hose to take the dust out of the pores. Go to #600 grit and possibly beyond with a micromesh fabric commonly used on glass. Many times this is my final finish with the addition of a light layer of finishing wax.

After sanding, it is time to oil the wood. We use an oil mix called Nelsonite, but there are many good oils on the market and many mixes that can be experimented with.

Small pieces are usually soaked in a 5-gallon can and let drain over a sink. Be sure to catch the drips below and reuse the oil. If the wood is very oily to begin with, like rosewoods, one treatment is usually enough.

We dry the piece after a short while with old T-shirts — all-cotton works best. For larger pieces, use 4/0 steel wool or a rag to apply the oil. Allow this to dry for one or two days. The wood should be dry and not sticky. Make sure it is wiped off well and that no globs are visible.

We use this method on furniture also, but continue on with four to six coats of oil. Each time lighter and lighter applications are used so that the oil sinks in evenly, and there are no dry spots.

This next part we have learned from Jeff Seaton, who graciously shared this method with us. He still creates the best finish I've ever seen.

We set up a buffing pad using a lambs wool pad and a medium stiff black rubber-backing disc. This is mounted on the end of a motor, 1/3 horse is fine — an old refrigerator or washing machine motor works. Now we apply red or yellow tripoli. This is a jewelers type rouge for removing the finest hairs raised by the oiling. Finally, we change the pad to avoid contamination and apply carnuba wax. Avoid using too much wax — test with scrap pieces of wood. This is not difficult, but it requires some practice.

On furniture, we don't use the tripoli or wax. I think the oil finish is much deeper and clearer because there is virtually nothing on top of the wood.

Subtractive art is what we do — taking away — the "art" is what remains. In Japanese art and culture, there is an emphasis called *Ma*, for example. In certain plays (called no plays), a small drum is struck and the beat is followed by silence and repeated always with the silence. This is unlike a pause or rest characteristic of western music, but even with no sound, something vital remains. And so to the Japanese, *Ma* is not an empty space, but rather it is the space that remains. It is the necessary interval to give shape to the whole.

CRITERIA

There has been a lot of discussion about what woodworkers do. Is woodworking an art or is it a craft? Does it count only if you do it yourself or is it okay to work in a group?

The making of an object is an interactive process. It is you and the wood — you can battle it out or go with the flow — it is not a one-way situation.

You can work this material to make a living, to fill up your time, or to test your skills and learn something new. You can do it with 10 people and a computer or by hand in your basement. It's your decision and your priorities.

And, if it's art — I guess it might rattle some cages or soothe a beast or evoke some emotion. It might be the simplest little box that's done so right and feels so tight that it makes someone smile.

This leads me to the idea of having some criteria for the work at hand. It's not really something you have to be tied to 100 percent, but a guide or structure.

Here is a four-point picture that was shown to me by John Schaeffer of Real Goods Trading Company. Initially, there are questions to be asked. What do I do? If you are a practicing craftsman, setting some criteria might keep you on a steady path. What do I want to accomplish? This might be the question for a new project or totally new venture.

These are the criteria I use most often:

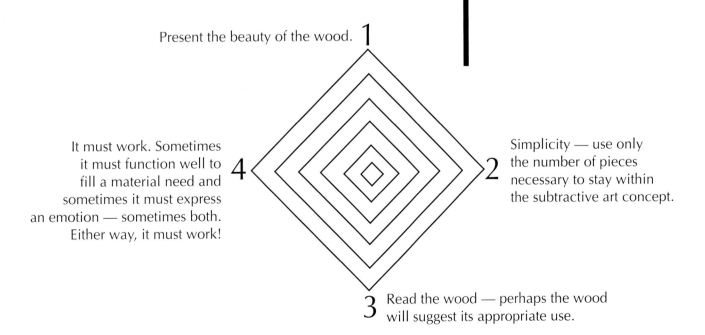

Present the beauty of the wood. **1**

It must work. Sometimes it must function well to fill a material need and sometimes it must express an emotion — sometimes both. Either way, it must work! **4**

2 Simplicity — use only the number of pieces necessary to stay within the subtractive art concept.

3 Read the wood — perhaps the wood will suggest its appropriate use.

This is just the beginning. Declare your own criteria, break the mold, abuse the formula.

Let me give you an example of a piece I did where the criteria was not followed. I had an idea to do a wine rack, and I thought that if I used just two sides with some support pieces it could be used on a table, or as a table. I wound up with six pieces of wood, and since I had to cut holes in the biggest piece in order to accommodate the bottles, I was left with a bunch of skinny boards of which none really showed the wood. So I went back and thought about my own criteria.

First, I didn't really present the wood very well. It wasn't very simple, although somewhat subtractive; I had to use six pieces to do it. I did use the appropriate wood, but since you couldn't see the grain, it didn't matter much. As a whole, it worked functionally, but only one of the four criteria was met.

Now look at one of the most simple pieces I make — the oval mirror box. Using a special piece of wood for the lid presents the beauty of the wood. It is very simple. Two pieces, subtracting wood from the inside of both, we created a box and a lid. "Reading the wood" allows us to use the appropriate grain patterns for both the lid and the bottom. It is functional; it is both a mirror and a box, and if we're lucky, perhaps evokes an emotion.

Desk blocks

PART FOUR

The
Galleries

VENUES
FOR
THE
WORK

Through the years, from the very beginning, galleries have been the very best venue for my work. Many have been supportive for the 16 years I've worked wood.

I believe the galleries have been instrumental in creating a new genre of expression in America. The public acceptance of craft as art can be directly attributed to the galleries' willingness to take chances.

"Michael and Friends" —
a show at the
Real Mother Goose Gallery
Portland, Oregon

Real Mother Goose Gallery

Michael is drawn to beauty like a moth is drawn to a flame. Unlike the moth, it is Michael who consumes and is revitalized. He draws his strength and inspiration from beauty in his environment, relationships, and the objects he creates. Michael seems to think of his work as a partnership with nature. His role in the partnership is to eloquently reveal the grandeur that nature provides. The clean lines of his designs and the quality of his workmanship are a statement of his respect for his chosen medium.

Appalachian Spring has shown Michael's work on a continual basis since the early 1980s. Like any seeker, he is always exploring his medium. When we first met, his work consisted primarily of small maple burl boxes. Since that time, he has added sculpture, furniture, and a variety of office accessories, as well as his "smart wood" program. It is a delight to have so closely followed his career, seen the growth, and continued to be associated with his fine studio. We look forward to the future with Michael, never knowing what it will bring, but knowing it will be great!

— Paula & David Brooks
Appalachian Spring
Washington, D.C.

GALLERY WORKS

I feel at home in the woods, the sun streaming through the trees, creating a dapple of colors in the fall. The rustling of the undergrowth, as I walk through the forest. There is so much life under these trees. I have identified 30 types of mushrooms alone. It is amazing and fascinating. We've lived in this little clearing for 23 years now. We've experienced this virtual rain forest, through the changing seasons. Watching the creek rise almost three feet in early spring and slowly changing its course through the woods. The hemlocks growing on downed trees in the soil created from others that have rotted away.

Philadelphia, 1950

Stairway

Like my ancestors, I use my eyes and my hands. The eyes to observe nature for form, for material, for function. It is from nature that my creativity derives. The connection with the object and natural phenomenon is constant, rigorous, and faithful. The hands are for defining — shaped, polished, and chiseled — to be re-seen in concrete form so as to be compared with the memory that inspired.

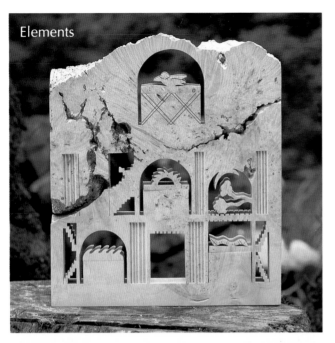

Elements

Rainbow

Tower of Tunnels

The Butterfly — wall-hung, maple burl, nesting boxes within. This is a collaboration with Helen Issifu.

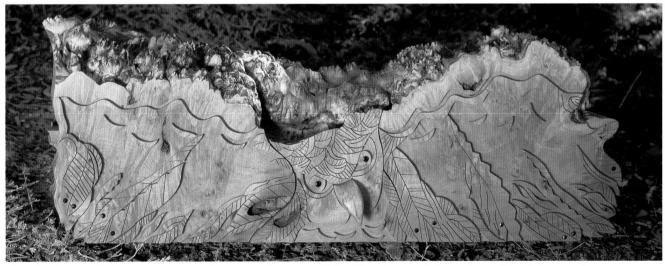

The Owl — wall-hung, maple burl, nesting boxes within. This is a collaboration with Helen Issifu.

Small Sculptural Paperweights

The Path Home

Wolfman. Maple burl. This is a collaboration with Helen Issifu.

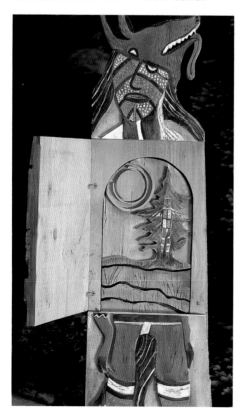

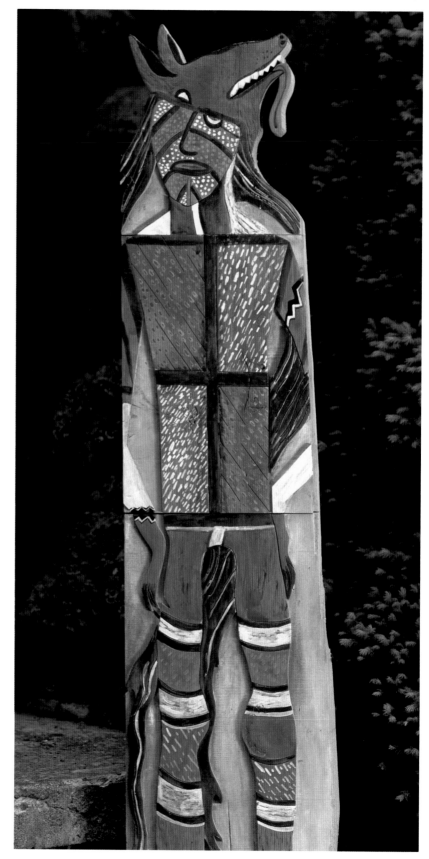

Bird's Nest. This is a collection of
Lewis Judy and Toni Gilbert.

Tower of Wings

The Castle Series

124

I opened the box
and saw the birthright:
backbones that seized the forest
with an air of ancient possession,
that lofted shoulder stretches
    of branch
into clean palates of sunlight,
that sent spirited syrup flowing
    into veins
beneath furrowed black bark.
I closed the box.

I opened the box
and reached down to brail the burl:
here lay no vestigial tail of tree,
no afterthought knotted into timber.
Here rested rootful essence
plaited into braids,
a shroud of memory
stitched into everlastingness.
I closed the box.

I opened the box
to a sound that swayed like
    a metronome:
"Redeem me from descent
into brimstone and ash,
salvage me from haunted places.
Carve me deep as the sea caves
and render me sheenful as
    water folds.
Listen now to my redemption song."
I could not close the box.

          — Woody Rudin

There are those who
believe we have dominion
over the Earth and those
who believe we are the
caretakers. Sometimes the
difference is great and
sometimes it is minuscule,
but without the beauty
of nature, we are lost.

INDEX